CUSTER BATTLEFIELD NATIONAL MONUMENT

CUSTER BATTLEFIELD
NATIONAL MONUMENT · MONTANA

ROBERT M. UTLEY

OFFICE OF PUBLICATIONS

NATIONAL PARK SERVICE

U.S. DEPARTMENT OF THE INTERIOR

WASHINGTON, D. C. 1969

CUSTER BATTLEFIELD

HISTORICAL HANDBOOK SERIES No. 1

The publication of this handbook was made possible by a grant from the Custer Battlefield Historical and Museum Association, Inc.

This publication is one of a series of handbooks describing the historical and archeological areas in the National Park System administered by the National Park Service, U.S. Department of the Interior.

CONTENTS

A CUSTER PROFILE 8

A CUSTER PROFILE

George Armstrong Custer is one of the most controversial figures in American history. In his associates he inspired either love or hate, but never indifference. History has reflected this disagreement. Some historians have characterized him as reckless, brutal, egotistical, selfish, unprincipled, and immature. Others have viewed him as portrayed by his first biographer: a model of "truth and sincerity, honor and bravery, tenderness, sympathy, unassuming piety and temperance." And still others have seen in him, both as a soldier and as a person, a paradoxical combination of virtue and vice.

Graduating from West Point in 1861 at the foot of his class, the young lieutenant plunged into the Civil War with an aggressive fighting spirit that within 2 years brought him to the attention of his superiors. In 1863 Gen. Alfred Pleasanton selected him and two other youthful officers for promotion to high rank. At the age of 23 Custer became a brigadier general, the youngest in the U.S. Army since Lafayette; 2 years later he won his second star. From Gettysburg to Appomattox, the dashing, gold-bedecked horseman led first the Michigan Cavalry Brigade and then the Third Cavalry Division from one triumph to another. By the close of the war he was a trusted lieutenant of General Sheridan and a widely admired national hero.

Although a major general of volunteers and a major general by brevet in the Regular Army, Custer's rank in the Army line had by 1865 advanced only to captain. With the reorganization of the Regular Army in 1866, however, he received the rank of lieutenant colonel of the newly formed 7th Cavalry Regiment. For the next 10 years, while the colonel of the regiment was kept on detached service, Custer led the 7th in campaigns against the Sioux, Cheyenne, Arapaho, Comanche, and Kiowa Indians of the Great Plains. His most celebrated victory was the Battle of the Washita in November 1868, when he surprised and destroyed Black Kettle's Cheyenne village. When death ended his career in 1876, the yellow-haired cavalryman was only 36 years old.

In 1864 Custer married Elizabeth Bacon of Monroe, Mich. The devotion of the couple became legendary, and "Libbie" followed her husband from one remote frontier station to another during his Plains service. In 1867 Custer's zeal to see his wife prompted him to leave his command in the field and travel nearly 300 miles to the fort where she awaited him. For this and other alleged offenses, he was tried by court-martial and suspended from rank and command for a year. After the Little Bighorn disaster, Mrs. Custer wrote several interesting books about frontier Army life and survived her husband by 57 years. She died in 1933 at the age of 91.

On a hot June Sunday in 1876, hordes of painted Indian warriors—perhaps as many as 4,000—swarmed over a treeless Montana ridge rising from the Little Bighorn River Valley. Five companies of U.S. Cavalry, about 215 blue-shirted troopers, contended briefly and hopelessly against overwhelming odds. When the guns fell silent and the smoke and dust of battle lifted, every soldier lay dead.

This was "Custer's Last Stand"—the most spectacular triumph of the American Indian in his four-century struggle against the relentlessly advancing European civilization that finally crushed him. It forms a chapter of American history that has inspired intense study and provoked intense controversy, that has been chronicled endlessly in prose and verse and enacted time and again on motion picture and television screens, and that has earned a lasting place in the Nation's historical annals and popular folklore. In total defeat and death, Custer and his men achieved an immortality that even the most dramatic victory could not have won them.

After the close of the Civil War, the Nation resumed its westward march. An army of workmen pushed the rails of the Union Pacific up the Platte River Valley, to meet and join in 1869 with the Central Pacific beyond the Rocky Mountains. The Northern Pacific built from St. Paul, aiming for Dakota Territory and ultimately the Pacific Northwest. Steamers worked up the Missouri River, carrying passengers and freight to Fort Benton for the land journey to the gold mines of western Montana. Along the railroad and steamboat routes, the U.S. Army built forts and stationed troops to guard travelers and settlers.

Between the Platte on the south, the Missouri on the east and north, and the Rockies on the west dwelled several powerful Indian tribes. In numbers, wealth, and warlike inclination, none surpassed the seven tribes of Teton Sioux that roamed the buffalo plains stretching westward from the Missouri to the foothills of the Bighorn Mountains. Frequently allied with the

Maj. Gen. George A. Custer

Sioux were the less numerous but equally warlike Northern Cheyennes. In 1866 the Sioux and Northern Cheyennes reacted violently to the white man's attempt to open a road through the western half of this domain. They had recently wrested the Powder River country from the Crow tribe and had no desire to see it overrun with gold seekers hastening to the Montana diggings. For 2 years, even though the Army built three guardian forts, the Sioux made travel on the Bozeman Trail a dangerous and often fatal undertaking.

The Red Cloud War ended in 1868 with the Fort Laramie Treaty. The Indians thought they had won, for the hated forts were abandoned, the road closed, the Powder River country guaranteed as unceded hunting grounds, and all of present South Dakota west of the Missouri set aside as the Great Sioux Reservation. But the treaty also contained the seeds of their ruin, for it bound the Sioux to settle on the vast new reservation. Free rations lured many to the agencies at once. Others, following the example of the proud chieftain Sitting Bull, remained in the unceded hunting range, determined never to fall under the white man's domination.

The latter groups soon acquired the label "hostiles"; they occasionally committed depredations on the Montana settlements and openly fought the military units that escorted Northern Pacific Railroad surveyors into the Yellowstone River Valley in 1872 and 1873. The former groups, the "friendlies," accepted Government control and gathered at agencies on the Missouri and White Rivers. Between hostiles and friendlies, however, there was much mobility; as families tired of one life, they set forth to try the other.

The Sioux had fought the Red Cloud War simply to prevent white prospectors from tramping across their country to the Montana goldfields. Now from the very heart of their country came rumors of gold deposits sparkling in the clear streams of the Black Hills. These forested, game-rich slopes lay within the Great Sioux Reservation, guaranteed to the Indians by the Treaty of 1868. But in 1874 a dramatic confirmation of

One of Custer's scouts

the rumors set off a rush to the new bonanza. Vainly the Army tried to turn back the gold seekers, and vainly the Government sought to buy the Black Hills from the Sioux.

The Black Hills episode catalyzed the discontent that had smoldered on both sides since 1868. The Sioux justly charged the Government with breaking the Fort Laramie Treaty by permitting encroachment on Indian land and by failing to provide at the agencies all the goods and services promised. The whites justly charged the Sioux with breaking the treaty by raiding the settlements and travel routes fringing the Indian domain. As the Powder River bands swelled with discontented agency Sioux in 1875, the Government laid plans to end their troublesome aggressions and, perhaps in the process, frighten the agency chiefs into selling the Black Hills.

So long as the Indians did not have to depend on the Government for food, they could not be fully controlled. And so long as they had access to the abundant game resources of the unceded hunting grounds, they would not be dependent. Late in December 1875, therefore, swift native runners left the Sioux agencies bearing an ultimatum from the Commissioner of Indian Affairs to the Powder River bands: report at the agencies by January 31, 1876, or be classified as hostiles subject to military action. That the deadline allowed insufficient time for the move or that it was midwinter made little difference. The chiefs did not take the message seriously and made no effort to comply. On February 1, 1876, the Secretary of the Interior certified the Indians in the unceded territory as hostile and asked the Secretary of War to take such measures as he thought appropriate.

Campaign of 1876

In Chicago Lt. Gen. Philip H. Sheridan, whose Division of the Missouri included the Sioux country, welcomed this decision. He had advocated a winter campaign that would catch the Sioux off guard and had fretted over the delay caused by the Indian Bureau's insistence on first giving them a chance to come in. At once Sheridan ordered his department commanders, Brig. Gen. George Crook in Omaha and Brig. Gen. Alfred H. Terry

Brig. Gen. George Crook

in St. Paul, to organize strong expeditions for an invasion of the enemy stronghold. The plan was for three columns, one from Crook's department and two from Terry's department, to converge from three directions on the locale thought to be occupied by the Indians. No particular concert of action was planned, for each column would be strong enough to defeat the 500 to 800 warriors the Indian Bureau estimated to be absent from the agencies.

Bad weather delayed General Terry's two columns, but General Crook, the "Gray Fox," at once organized an 800-man column, consisting of infantry and cavalry, at Fort Fetterman, Wyo. During early March he pushed northward on the old Bozeman Trail through deep snow and subzero cold. On March 17 a striking column of six cavalry companies, led by Col. J. J. Reynolds, assaulted a winter camp of Sioux and Cheyennes on Powder River. The surprised Indians scattered but mounted a counterattack that prompted the cautious Reynolds to abandon his gains and fall back on the main column. Crook turned about and headed for Fort Fetterman to outfit for another campaign.

As Crook reorganized at Fort Fetterman, Terry prepared his two commands, and in April and May 1876 Sheridan's three-pronged offensive, now a summer instead of a winter operation, at last got underway. Early in April Col. John Gibbon led the "Montana Column"—about 450 men of the 2d Cavalry and 7th Infantry Regiments—eastward from Fort Ellis, Mont., down the north bank of the Yellowstone River. On May 29 Crook's expedition again headed north from Fort Fetterman. And on May 17 the "Dakota Column" marched out of Fort Abraham Lincoln and, leaving the Missouri River behind, pointed toward the Yellowstone.

The Dakota Column included all 12 companies of the 7th Cavalry Regiment, two companies of the 17th Infantry and one of the 6th to guard a train of 150 wagons, a detachment of the 20th Infantry serving three rapid-fire Gatling guns, and about 40 Arikara Indian scouts. Altogether the Dakota Column num-

Chief Sitting Bull

bered about 925 officers and men. Although General Terry accompanied it, he expected the colorful commander of the 7th Cavalry to lead his horsemen in the swift thrust that would bring the enemy to battle. This was Lt. Col. George Armstrong Custer, a major general in the Civil War and now, at 36, a plainsman of 10 years experience. Custer and his regiment had fought Sitting Bull on the Yellowstone in 1873 and confirmed the existence of gold in the Black Hills in 1874. Now, as Terry's striking arm, they hoped for an opportunity to crush the power of the Sioux for all time.

Terry received no indication of the probable location of the hostiles until he reached the Yellowstone. At the mouth of the Powder River, he met officers from the Montana Column who reported that Colonel Gibbon's scouts had discovered an enemy camp in the valley of the Tongue River. Sending Maj. Marcus A. Reno and six companies of the 7th Cavalry on a southward swing to examine this valley further, Terry prepared to push on to meet the Montana Column.

At the mouth of the Powder, the general established a supply depot manned by his infantry and another three companies that had marched south from Fort Buford. Here, too, he met Capt. Grant Marsh with the river steamer *Far West,* chartered by the Government to transport supplies and speed communication. Leaving all his wagons at the depot and organizing a mule packtrain to carry provisions, Terry sent Custer up the river-bank and himself boarded the *Far West,* to steam to the mouth of Rosebud Creek, where Gibbon's troops lay in camp on the north side of the Yellowstone.

Custer and Reno reunited here on June 21. Reno had led his scouting force into the Rosebud Valley and discovered an Indian trail that confirmed Terry's suspicions: the hostiles were moving up this valley and would probably cross the Wolf Mountains into the valley of a stream that the Sioux called the Greasy Grass but that Army maps labeled the Little Bighorn.

Indian Movements

From General Sheridan down to the newest lieutenant, the

Maj. Marcus A. Reno

great worry was that the hostiles would evade the columns sent after them. Rarely, unless absolutely certain of victory, did the Plains Indian stand and fight; usually he faded into the hills and easily eluded his slow-moving pursuers. Thus military planning focused mainly on how to catch the quarry rather than on how to defeat him once caught. Sheridan's plans assumed that each of the converging columns could alone handle any gathering of hostiles it succeeded in bringing to battle. In all the unceded territory, according to the Indian Bureau, the warrior force did not exceed 800, and the possibility that these might unite in one place was not seriously considered.

As a matter of fact, a great many more Indians were absent from their agencies than the Bureau had reported, and they continued to flock to Sitting Bull's standard throughout the spring. By June the scattered bands had begun to come together in a single village that formed one of the largest in the history of the Great Plains. All the Teton Sioux were represented—Hunkpapas under Sitting Bull, Gall, Crow King, and Black Moon; Oglalas under Crazy Horse, Low Dog, and Big Road; the Miniconjou followers of Hump; Sans Arc, Blackfoot, and Brule Sioux. There were also Northern Cheyennes under Two Moon, Lame White Man, and Dirty Moccasins, and a handful of warriors from tribes of Eastern Sioux. They clustered around six separate tribal circles, and altogether they numbered perhaps 10,000 to 12,000 people, mustering a fighting force of between 2,500 and 4,000 men. Many had firearms—some the Winchester repeating rifle obtained, quite legally, from traders and Indian agents for hunting.

Secure in their unaccustomed numbers, the Sioux and Cheyennes, moving up Rosebud Creek in mid-June, wasted little thought on the news brought by some young men that they had seen soldiers farther south, beyond the head of the Rosebud. Turning west, the great procession crossed the Wolf Mountains and came to rest on a tributary of the Little Bighorn later named Reno Creek. Here further reports confirmed the presence of many soldiers descending the Rosebud, and more than a thousand warriors rode over the mountains to contest the advance.

On the morning of June 17, General Crook collided with this array, and after a severe action lasting most of the day he turned about and marched back to Goose Creek (near present Sheridan, Wyo.) to call for reinforcements. The Indians returned to their tepees in triumph and at once moved down Reno Creek, crossed the Little Bighorn, and laid out a new camp. It lined the west bank of the river for 3 miles and sprawled in places all the way across the mile-wide valley

The Battle of the Rosebud infused the Indians with confidence. And well it might, for it had thrown back one of Sheridan's columns and prevented its juncture with the others. Of the proximity of the others, however, the hostiles had no knowledge, while of their location the military commanders had formed a nearly correct idea. On the very day of the Battle of the Rosebud, Major Reno had examined the broad Indian trail in Rosebud Valley, and even as the Sioux and Cheyennes moved their village to the Little Bighorn, Terry, Gibbon, and Custer laid plans to smash it.

Plan of Action

On the evening of June 21 General Terry gathered his principal subordinates in the cabin of the *Far West,* moored to the bank of the Yellowstone at the mouth of the Rosebud, and worked out the details of a strategy that had already formed in his mind for snaring the Indians whose trail Reno had seen in the Rosebud Valley. Two fundamental assumptions shaped this plan: that the enemy probably numbered less than a thousand warriors, and that unless surrounded and forced into battle they would flee to the mountains as soon as they discovered the approach of soldiers. Although General Crook had learned that Sioux strength and will to fight had been grossly underestimated, word of his recent setback had not yet reached Terry.

Terry's information indicated that the hostile camp almost certainly lay somewhere in the Little Bighorn Valley. By maneuvering Custer into position on one side and Gibbon on

the other, he hoped to box in the Indians and force them into battle. Accordingly, Custer would lead his regiment up the Rosebud, cross to the Little Bighorn, and drop down that stream from the south; Gibbon, accompanied by Terry and his staff, would march back up the Yellowstone, ferry to the south bank, ascend the Bighorn, and enter the Little Bighorn Valley from the north.

Although recognizing that uncertainties of terrain and enemy location would prevent close cooperation, Terry hoped that no action would be precipitated before June 26—the earliest day Gibbon's foot soldiers could reach the objective. To afford Gibbon the needed time and to satisfy himself that the quarry had not slipped out of the trap to the southeast, Terry intended for Custer to continue up the Rosebud beyond the point where the hostile trail turned west and not veer toward the Little Bighorn until he had passed the head of the Rosebud.

Terry fully understood that Custer's cavalry, with no infantry to hold it back, enjoyed a much better chance of striking a blow than did Gibbon. For this reason he let Custer have six of Gibbon's Crow Indian scouts, who knew the country better than the Arikaras, and also offered to send along Gibbon's battalion of the 2d Cavalry under Maj. James Brisbin, as well as the Gatling gun battery. Custer gratefully accepted the scouts but declined the additional cavalry and the artillery. The Gatlings, he said in truth, would slow his march; Brisbin's cavalry, he explained less plausibly, would not enable him to overcome any opposition that the 7th alone could not cope with.

The next morning, June 22, Terry outlined his views to Custer in writing. Before sketching in general terms the troop movements that had been decided upon, the general noted the impossibility of giving definite instructions, and he professed, anyway, to repose too much confidence in his subordinate's "zeal, energy, and ability" to attempt to lay down detailed orders "which might hamper your action when nearly in contact with the enemy." Custer should conform to Terry's views, therefore, unless he saw "sufficient reason for departing from them." Depart from them he did. Whether sufficient reason existed has ever since been a topic of heated controversy.

March to the Little Bighorn

At noon on June 22 the 7th Cavalry passed in review for Terry and, behind the buckskin-clad Custer, began the march up the Rosebud. The column numbered 31 officers and about 585 enlisted men, 40 Indian scouts, and nearly 20 packers, guides, and other civilian employees. Each trooper carried 100 cartridges for his carbine and 24 for his pistol, and a mule packtrain transported another 50 rounds of carbine ammunition per man together with rations and forage for 15 days.

Amid clouds of choking dust, Custer's column pushed up the Rosebud. On the 23d it struck the hostile trail, which throughout the afternoon and all next day grew rapidly fresher and larger. In the broad trail and the proliferation of abandoned campsites, the Crow and Arikara scouts saw evidence of a great many more Indians than Custer and his officers suspected— perhaps several thousand—and they made no secret of their misgivings over being drawn into a fight with such an array.

Although Custer thought the scouts inclined to exaggerate, he had raised his own estimate of enemy strength to 1,500 warriors, a force he judged his regiment well able to handle. A different fear gripped him, as it had everyone from the beginning of the campaign—that the Sioux would escape if given a chance. Impelled by this likelihood, he pushed the column hard—from 12 miles on the 22d to 30 each on the 23d and 24th. By the evening of the 24th, he had reached the point where the trail bent to the west and ascended the divide between the Rosebud and Little Bighorn Valleys. Indian "sign" left little doubt that the Sioux village lay just over the mountains.

Here Custer made a crucial decision. Instead of continuing up the Rosebud as Terry desired, he would follow the trail nearly to the summit of the divide, spend the 25th resting his exhausted command and fixing the location of the hostile camp, then hit it with a dawn attack on the 26th, the date appointed for Gibbon to reach the mouth of the Little Bighorn.

A night march, adding 10 miles to the 30 already covered during the day, carried the regiment nearly to the summit At the same time, Lt. Charles A. Varnum and several of his scouts climbed a high hill to the south, known as the Crow's Nest, and at dawn scanned the wrinkled landscape stretching off to the Bighorn Mountains. Some 15 miles to the west, where a thread of green traced the course of the Little Bighorn, the Crows discerned smoke rising from the Sioux village and on the benchland beyond a vast undulating mass that represented the Sioux pony herd. Lieutenant Varnum could not see these things, and neither could Custer when he arrived in response to a message from the lieutenant.

Although doubting that his scouts had actually detected the village, Custer knew it could not be far off. Moreover, his worst fears at once seemed confirmed, for two small parties of Sioux were spotted during the morning. Unquestionably, the regiment had now been discovered. If action were delayed until the 26th as planned, there would probably be no Indians to attack. And so Custer made his second crucial decision—to find the village and strike it as soon as possible.

For his decisions on the evening of the 24th and the morning of the 25th, Custer's detractors, pointing to his burning pride in the 7th Cavalry and his reputation as an impetuous commander, have charged him with willful disobedience of orders springing from a blind determination to win all the glory. He failed to meet Terry's desire that he continue up the Rosebud beyond the point where the Indian trail left it before turning to the Little Bighorn, then rushed his exhausted command into battle a day early and without first ascertaining the location and strength of the enemy.

Custer's defenders have replied that Terry's instructions were not binding, that the hostile trail clearly revealed that the Sioux were so close that they could not possibly have slipped off to the southeast, and that to continue the march up the Rosebud would not only have been pointless but might have afforded them the opportunity to escape. Once the regiment had been

Chief Gall

discovered, moreover, there was no other proper decision than to attack, for the enemy could hardly have been expected to remain in place waiting until the soldiers found it convenient to fight.

A good case can be made for either point of view, and the imponderables insure that men will always arrive at different answers. The command decisions that brought on the Battle of the Little Bighorn will doubtless continue to form fascinating topics of debate.

Reno Attacks

Shortly after noon on June 25, 1876, the 7th Cavalry topped the divide and paused at the head of the stream that later took the name Reno Creek. Here Custer had his adjutant, Lt. W. W. Cooke, form the regiment into three battalions. Major Reno took command of one, consisting of Companies A, G, and M— perhaps as many as 140 men, although straggling later reduced the number somewhat. Capt. Frederick W. Benteen headed the second, consisting of Companies H, D, and K, about 125 men. Custer himself retained five companies, C, E, F, I, and L, about 215 men. Capt. Thomas McDougall was assigned with B Company to guard the packtrain.

Perhaps still conscious of Terry's strictures about preventing the flight of the hostiles to the southeast, Custer at once ordered Captain Benteen to lead his battalion in that direction, along the base of the Wolf Mountains, and to "pitch into anything he might find." As Benteen's column wheeled to the left, Custer and Reno, placing their battalions on opposite sides of the creek, took up the march down the narrow valley toward the Little Bighorn. The Indian scouts preceded the advance, and the packtrain followed in the rear.

A march of about 10 miles brought Custer and Reno, by 2:15 p.m., to within 4 miles of the Little Bighorn. Here, at an abandoned Sioux campsite, the troops flushed a party of about 40 warriors, who raced their ponies toward the river. Beyond, a great cloud of dust rose from behind a line of bluffs that hid the Little Bighorn Valley north of the mouth of Reno Creek.

Custer had now discovered the enemy. The dust probably signified to him that the village lay behind the bluffs and that its occupants were trying to get away. Even though Benteen could not be called upon, the situation demanded an immediate attack. Instantly, Custer ordered Reno to pursue the fleeing warriors, "and charge afterward, and you will be supported by the whole outfit."

At this point Custer may have intended to support Reno by following him into battle with the five companies under his personal leadership. As Reno's battalion and the Arikara scouts forded the river, however, they saw in the distance swarms of Indians apparently riding up the valley to give battle. Fred Gerard, a civilian interpreter, knew that Custer supposed the Indians to be fleeing. He turned back on the trail and overtook Lieutenant Cooke and another officer who had accompanied Reno as far as the river. Explaining that the Indians were not fleeing at all but were coming out to fight, Gerard wheeled to rejoin Reno.

Reno's battalion advanced down the Little Bighorn Valley at a trot. Two miles ahead lay the objective. A few tepees marking the upper end of the Sioux encampment could be faintly seen through the dust clouds. Horsemen in growing numbers swarmed forth from the village to meet the attack. Reno ordered a charge, and the line broke into a gallop. Anxiously the major looked back for the support Custer had promised, but none appeared. Another one-half mile and the soldiers would be swallowed by perhaps seven times their number of aggressive warriors. Reno threw up his hand and shouted the command to fight on foot.

Within sight of the first tepees of the village the charge ground to a halt. A thin skirmish line stretched part way across the valley. Mounted Sioux raced the length of the line, curled around the left flank, and appeared in the rear. Within 15 minutes the position had grown untenable. Reno flanked right into the timber, but in the heavy undergrowth he lost control of his companies. Warriors worked through the brush and trees and

gathered on the other side of the river to fire from the rear. Within half an hour, closely pressed and running low on ammunition, the major decided that the new position could not be held either.

The high bluffs across the river appeared to offer the only refuge from the encircling tribesmen. Reno ordered his men into the open, mounted them in a loose column formation, and led a charge toward the river. The retreat verged on a panic rout as masses of Sioux closed in on the handful of troopers. At the river no one organized a force to cover the crossing, and warriors clustered on the bank to fire at the struggling soldiers in the water. Those who reached the east side made their way up the ravines that cut into a rampart of bluffs rising steeply to a height of 300 feet above the water.

Exhausted and beaten, the remnant of the battalion gathered atop the bluffs. Of about 130 men who had entered the fight, 33 had been killed. Among them were Lt. Donald McIntosh, Lt. B. H. Hodgson, Dr. J. M. DeWolf, and the famed scout "Lonesome" Charley Reynolds. Many more were wounded, and Lt. C. C. DeRudio and 16 men were missing. They had not heard the order to retreat and had been left in the timber. Fortunately for them and for the survivors on Reno Hill, the Indians almost immediately relaxed the pressure, and soon they had seemingly withdrawn altogether.

It was now late afternoon, perhaps shortly after 4 p.m. Knots of officers and men anxiously speculated over the whereabouts of Custer.

The Annihilation of Custer

No man can know with certainty how Custer's battalion met its fate, for no member of it survived. From the confused and contradictory accounts of the Indian participants and from the placement of the bodies on the battlefield, the movements of the contending forces can be roughly reconstructed. But the details of the action, together with Custer's intentions and the factors which shaped them, must ever remain a mystery.

Major Reno had expected Custer to follow him into battle.

Capt. Frederick W. Benteen

Why Custer instead turned north from Reno's trail may only be surmised. He may not have intended to provide support in the way Reno expected, or he may have intended to but changed his mind when Adjutant Cooke brought word that the Indians were advancing to meet Reno. It may only be surmised, too, what Custer hoped to accomplish by his northward march. Did he plan to fall on the enemy's rear as Reno engaged the front? Or was he still obsessed with the fear that the Sioux would escape and took this means to block their route? Or did he entertain both thoughts? It should be borne in mind that, although warned by his scouts of unexpectedly large numbers of Indians in his front, Custer had not yet seen any part of the great village and knew with certainty no more of its size and location than suggested by the dust clouds toward which he now turned.

Shortly after taking the new direction of march, Custer sent Sgt. Daniel Kanipe back on the trail to find Captain McDougall and tell him to hasten forward with the ammunition mules. After a gallop of a mile or so, the battalion paused while Custer rode to the crest of the bluff. Tepees carpeted the valley below—it was his first view of the Indian village—and Reno was probably just going into action. Resuming the march, the column started down a long ravine emptying into Medicine Tail Coulee. During the descent, Custer summoned his orderly, Giovanni Martini, and sent him with another message for Benteen. Adjutant Cooke scrawled it on a page torn from his memorandum book: "Benteen. Come on. Big Village. Be Quick. Bring packs. W.W. Cooke. P.S. Bring pacs."

As Martini galloped back up the trail, he saw the battalion turn toward the river. Martini's glimpse is history's last view of Custer and his 215 cavalrymen in life. Whether part or all of them reached the river at the mouth of Medicine Tail Coulee is not known. If Custer intended to cross the river, here was a likely place—one in fact that would have placed him right in the center of the Indian camp.

But hordes of Sioux warriors under Chief Gall poured across

the stream at this ford and, either near the mouth of Medicine Tail Coulee or farther back on the slope dividing it from Deep Coulee, collided with the troops. Deflected to the right, the battalion fought successive rearguard actions toward a long ridge to the north. More warriors forded the river behind Gall. Others crossed still farther down. And Crazy Horse started down the valley with another large force, crossed the river, and swept round in a great arc that brought him ultimately to the battle ridge from the north.

Caught in rough terrain unsuited to mounted action and surrounded by overwhelming numbers of Sioux and Cheyenne warriors, the battalion swiftly disintegrated. The companies seem to have made individual stands, fighting on foot against the waves of Indians that rolled in from every direction. L Company, commanded by Custer's brother-in-law, Lt. James Calhoun, spread over the south end of the battle ridge. Capt. Myles Keogh and Company I were overrun on the east slope of the ridge. On the west, near the river, C and E Companies, under Capt. Thomas W. Custer and Lt. A. E. Smith, slipped into a deep ravine and were crushed. Company F, Capt. George W. Yates, straddled the center of the ridge, And at the north end, where Crazy Horse cut off further retreat, a knot of about 50 men gathered around Custer and his red and blue personal pennant, shot their horses for breastworks, and made their "last stand."

The fight probably opened shortly after 4 p.m., just as Reno reached the refuge of the bluffs. Probably by 5 p.m. not a man of Custer's battalion remained alive. (Today white marble headstones dot the battle ridge and its slopes. They show where the cavalrymen fell under the irresistible onslaught of the Sioux and Cheyenne warriors. How must be left largely to the imagination.)

Reno Besieged

Captain Benteen's march had revealed no sign of Indians, and at length he had turned back to the trail made by Custer and Reno, reaching it just in advance of Captain McDougall and the slow-moving packtrain. Here Sergeant Kanipe galloped up with the message from Custer to hasten forward with the packs. Benteen sent him to McDougall. A little later Trumpeter Martini, his horse bleeding from a bullet wound, arrived with the penciled order from Cooke to bring the packs and be quick.

The column pushed rapidly down Reno Creek, approaching the Little Bighorn in time to witness the last of Reno's men retreating from the valley. Some of the Crow scouts, whom Custer had released a short time before, directed Benteen to the bluffs on his right, where the remnant of Reno's battalion had gathered. A brief gallop united Benteen's troops with Reno's broken command on top of the bluffs. A short time later the packtrain and its escort labored into the defense lines that Benteen had swiftly formed.

The troops gathered on Reno Hill heard heavy and continuous firing from downstream. Two distinct volleys echoed over the hills. Certain that Custer was engaged, Capt. Thomas B. Weir urged Reno to ride to his support. The major refused, and without authority Weir went by himself, his company following under Lieutenant Edgerly. Later, the rest of the command strung out on Weir's trail. Topping the high pinnacle now known as Weir Point, Weir saw the Custer battlefield 3 miles in the distance, but smoke and dust obscured all details of the activity taking place there. Hundreds of warriors ascending the north slope of Weir Point halted the advance. After a brief skirmish, the soldiers fell back to Reno Hill. Mounting numbers of Sioux pressed from behind, swiftly surrounded the 350 or more troopers and packers, and at once brought them under a deadly fire that did not subside until twilight, 3 hours later.

Nightfall interrupted the siege, and most of the Indians returned to the village for a great war dance illuminated by leaping bonfires. On Reno Hill, the men spent the night digging shallow rifle pits and improvising breastworks from packs and dead animals. The defenses occupied a perimeter enclosing a shallow depression, in which Dr. H. R. Porter, a civilian under army contract, placed his hospital. Major Reno held the north

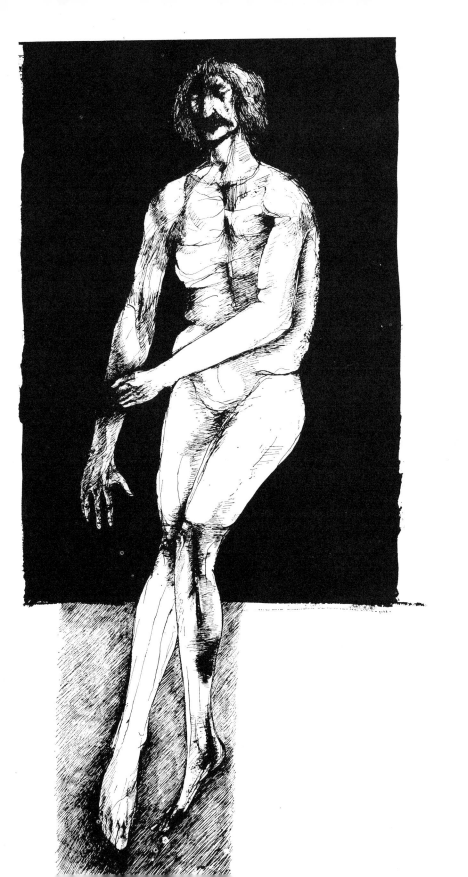

rim with most of the companies. Benteen occupied the south side, an elliptical ridge, with H Company. On the west, the bluffs dropped steeply to the Little Bighorn. On the east a gradual slope fell away to Reno Creek.

With the first hint of dawn, a single rifle shot signaled the resumption of the siege. From all sides the Indians poured a constant stream of arrows and bullets into the defense perimeter. The soldiers responded whenever a target offered itself, but the warriors were adept at drawing fire without getting hit.

Throughout the hot morning the fight continued without letup. The Indians worked themselves ever closer around the lines, taking advantage of the irregular terrain and clumps of sagebrush to avoid exposure. At times they threatened to mass for an attack, especially on Benteen's exposed and thinly held position. The captain strode about in full view, refusing to take cover and disdaining the deadly fire directed at him. On one occasion he roused his men to their feet and led them in a charge that broke up a cluster of warriors preparing for an assault. On another he went to Reno and demanded a general counterattack. Led by the major, the troopers rose from their pits and surged forward to drive back the encircling Sioux and Cheyennes.

Thirst tormented the defenders, especially the wounded in Dr. Porter's hospital. The surgeon served notice that his charges must have water at any hazard. Four sharpshooters stood up to distract the enemy and provide covering fire while a volunteer party slipped down a ravine to the river, filled canteens and camp kettles, and hastened back to the hill. They got little water, but it was enough to afford some relief to the wounded. For this feat, 19 men later received the Congressional Medal of Honor.

Early in the afternoon the siege relaxed, and by late afternoon only an occasional shot reminded the defenders to stay under cover. In the valley, the Indians fired the dry prairie grass. A wall of thick smoke screened the village from view. About 7 p.m. an immense procession of horsemen, women and children on foot, travois, ponies, and dogs emerged from behind the smoke. Slowly it wound up the slope on the west side of the valley and made its way across the benchland to the southwest, toward the peaks of the Bighorn Mountains. Below, the valley appeared deserted save for scattered debris of the great Indian camp.

Rescue

On Reno Hill the cavalrymen watched the exodus from the valley and speculated on its meaning. None knew what had happened to Custer. None knew why the Indians were leaving. None could shake the fear that the next morning would bring fresh waves of warriors against the hilltop. During the night the troops buried their dead and moved closer to the river. Lieutenant DeRudio and most of the soldiers and scouts left in the timber the day before made their way into the lines. They had remained concealed for a harrowing 36 hours while Indians came and went nearby.

Next morning a blue column was seen marching up the valley. Some thought it was Custer at last. Others thought it Terry. A few speculated that it was Crook. Two officers rode out to investigate. A short gallop brought them to the leading ranks of the 2d Cavalry, General Terry in the van. Both general and lieutenants burst out with the same question: "Where is Custer?"

Lt. James H. Bradley brought the answer. He and his Crow scouts had counted 197 bodies, most of them stripped of clothing and badly mutilated, littering the battle ridge 4 miles downstream. Custer's body lay just below the crest at the north end of the ridge. It had been stripped but neither scalped nor mutilated. One bullet had lodged in the left breast, another in the left temple.

Of about 215 officers and men in Custer's battalion, not one had survived—although the failure to find all the bodies left a faint possibility that someone may have escaped. In Reno's retreat from the valley and defense of the bluffs, another 47 men had been slain and 53 wounded. Altogether, half the regiment

lay dead or wounded. How many Indians paid for this victory with their lives will never be known, for the dead were borne off by the living. Estimates vary from 30 to 300.

On the morning of June 28, Reno's 7th Cavalrymen rode to the Custer battlefield for the sad chore of interring the dead. Tools were few, and in most cases the burial details simply scooped out a shallow grave and covered the body with a thin layer of sandy soil and some clumps of sagebrush. The officers were buried more securely and the graves plainly marked for future identification.

Meanwhile, Gibbon's troops improvised hand litters to carry Reno's wounded the 15 miles to the mouth of the Little Big-horn, where they were to be placed on the *Far West* and transported to Fort Lincoln. The hand litters proved too awkward and on the 29th were replaced with mule litters. On the morning of June 30 Captain Marsh received the wounded on the steamer deck, where they were laid on a bed of freshly cut grass.

Cautiously Captain Marsh piloted the *Far West* down the shallow Bighorn to its mouth, paused for 2 days awaiting Terry and Gibbon, then ferried the command to the north side of the Yellowstone. On July 3 Marsh eased his craft into the muddy current for an epic voyage that would become legendary in the history of river steamboating. Down the Yellowstone and Missouri the vessel sped. At 11 p.m. on July 5, draped in black mourning cloth, the *Far West* nosed into the Bismarck landing. Marsh had set a speed record never to be topped on the Missouri—710 miles in 54 hours.

The crew ran about the town spreading word of the Custer disaster. Captain Marsh hastened to the telegraph office, where the operator, J. M. Carnahan, seated himself at the key and tapped out a terse message confirming the rumors that had already begun to filter across the Nation. It was the first of a series of dispatches that by the end of the next day totaled 50,000 words.

Meanwhile, the *Far West* dropped down to Fort Lincoln. The wounded were carried ashore and placed in the post hospital. In the predawn gloom of July 6, officers went from house to

Capt. Myles W. Keogh

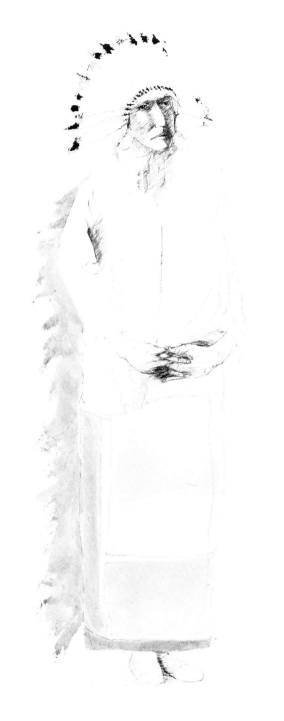

house rousing the occupants from bed and breaking the tragic news to the widows of the officers and men who had fallen with Custer.

Collapse of the Sioux

After the Battle of the Little Bighorn, the great Sioux and Cheyenne village broke up, the various bands going their separate ways to avoid the soldiers. A shocked and outraged Nation demanded that the slayers of Custer be punished, and soon heavy reinforcements poured up the Missouri.

Throughout the summer the columns of Terry and Crook searched for the hostiles but could bring on no important engagement. By autumn, however, many of the Indian fugitives had tired of the pursuit and, with winter coming on, slipped back to the agencies to surrender. The rest endured months of insecurity as troops braved the perils of a Montana winter to continue the campaign. Several times sleeping camps of Indians awoke to the crash of rifle and carbine fire and the sight of bluecoats among their tepees. With the approach of spring, hundreds drifted into the agencies and gave up. Even Crazy Horse saw the futility of holding out longer. On May 6, 1877, he led a procession of more than 1,100 Sioux into Camp Robinson, Nebr., and laid down his rifle.

Vowing never to accept reservation restraints, Sitting Bull and some 400 Hunkpapa Sioux crossed into Canada. But food was scarce and U.S. soldiers patroled the international boundary, preventing the Indians from hunting buffalo in Montana. Little by little the refugees weakened. First Gall, then Crow King led their followers to Fort Buford to surrender. Finally, in July 1881, Sitting Bull and 43 families appeared at the fort and gave up.

Sitting Bull's surrender formally marked the end of a war that had all but ended 4 years earlier, when the bulk of the hostiles of 1876 had settled on the reservations. In their triumph at the Little Bighorn, the Sioux and Cheyennes had awakened forces that led to their collapse. The Campaign of 1876 had, after all, accomplished the objectives set by its authors. It had compelled the Indians to abandon the unceded hunting grounds and accept Government control on the reservations. And it had frightened the chiefs into selling the Black Hills.

Bitterly the Sioux and Cheyennes submitted to the reservation way of life. Although it contrasted cruelly with the old life, gradually they came to see that the freedom of the past could never be recaptured. For a generation to come, however, old warriors would recall with satisfaction the brief moment of glory when they wiped out Custer's cavalry.

Custer Battlefield Today

Almost at once the scene of Custer's defeat became an important tourist attraction. Army officers and even Indian veterans of the battle visited it from time to time, and many Easterners en route to Yellowstone National Park or the Pacific Northwest on the newly built Northern Pacific Railway took time to journey up the Bighorn and Little Bighorn to view the historic spot. Troops from Fort Custer, established at the mouth of the Little Bighorn in 1877, served as the first custodians.

One year after the battle, Keogh's old company of the 7th Cavalry returned to the field, carefully reburied the dead where they had fallen, and placed wooden stakes over each grave. The bodies of 11 officers and two civilians were exhumed and shipped to the homes of relatives for reburial. Custer's remains were reinterred with impressive ceremony at West Point Military Academy, N.Y., on October 10, 1877. The grave is prominently located near the Old Cadet Chapel and is designated by a large but dignified marker.

A log memorial erected in 1879, when the battlefield was designated a National Cemetery, stood atop Custer Hill for 2 years. It was replaced in 1881 with the present granite monument bearing the names of those killed in the battle. The remains of the soldiers were then gathered from their individual graves and reinterred in a common grave around the base of the memorial. In subsequent years the wooden stakes indicating the places where the soldiers fell and were originally buried were replaced with white marble markers.

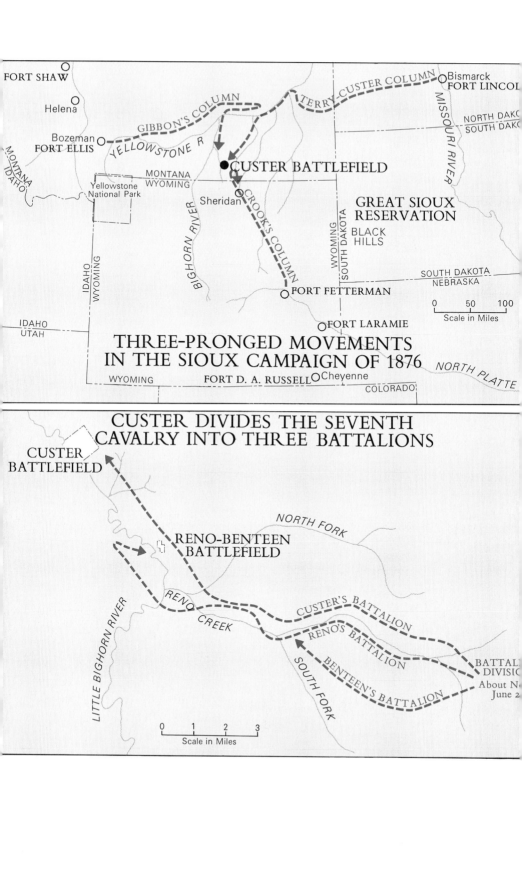

FORT SHAW ○

Helena ○

GIBBON'S COLUMN

Bozeman ○
FORT ELLIS

YELLOWSTONE R

MONTANA
IDAHO

Yellowstone
National Park

MONTANA
WYOMING

TERRY-CUSTER COLUMN

Bismarck ○
FORT LINCOL

MISSOURI RIVER

NORTH DAKO
SOUTH DAKO

●CUSTER BATTLEFIELD

Sheridan ○

CROOK'S COLUMN

BIGHORN RIVER

GREAT SIOUX
RESERVATION

WYOMING
SOUTH DAKOTA

BLACK
HILLS

IDAHO
WYOMING

SOUTH DAKOTA
NEBRASKA

○ FORT FETTERMAN

0   50   100
Scale in Miles

IDAHO
UTAH

○ FORT LARAMIE

THREE-PRONGED MOVEMENTS
IN THE SIOUX CAMPAIGN OF 1876

WYOMING   FORT D. A. RUSSELL ○ Cheyenne

NORTH PLATTE

COLORADO

CUSTER DIVIDES THE SEVENTH
CAVALRY INTO THREE BATTALIONS

CUSTER
BATTLEFIELD

NORTH FORK

RENO-BENTEEN
BATTLEFIELD

RENO CREEK

CUSTER'S BATTALION

RENO'S BATTALION

LITTLE BIGHORN RIVER

SOUTH FORK

BENTEEN'S BATTALION

BATTAL
DIVISIO
About N
June 2

0   1   2   3
Scale in Miles

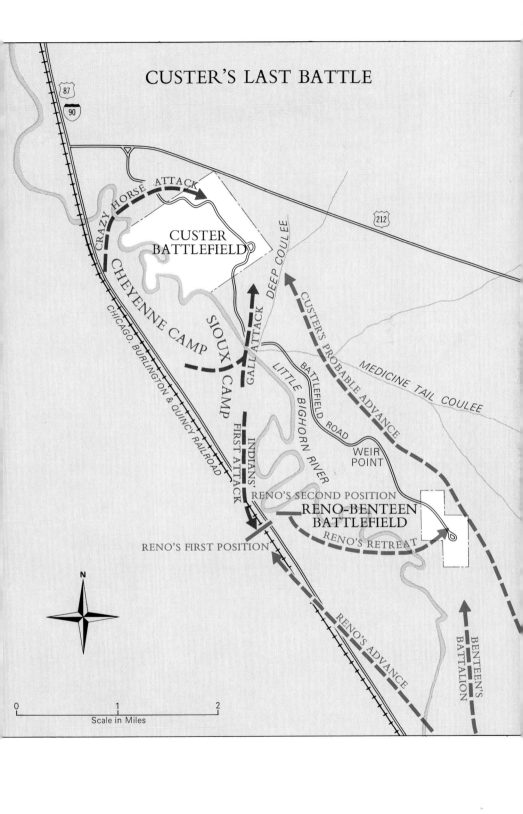

CUSTER'S LAST BATTLE

CUSTER
BATTLEFIELD

CRAZY HORSE ATTACK

CHEYENNE CAMP

SIOUX CAMP

GALL ATTACK

DEEP COULEE

CUSTER'S PROBABLE ADVANCE

MEDICINE TAIL COULEE

BATTLEFIELD ROAD

LITTLE BIGHORN RIVER

CHICAGO, BURLINGTON & QUINCY RAILROAD

INDIANS' FIRST ATTACK

WEIR POINT

RENO'S SECOND POSITION

RENO-BENTEEN
BATTLEFIELD

RENO'S RETREAT

RENO'S FIRST POSITION

RENO'S ADVANCE

BENTEEN'S BATTALION

N

0   1   2
Scale in Miles

APPENDIXES

I. Officers of the 7th Cavalry at the Battle of the Little Bighorn.
(Asterisks mark those killed in action.)

*Lt. Col. George A. Custer, commanding

Maj. Marcus A. Reno

*1st Lt.William W. Cooke, adjutant

*Assistant Surgeon George E. Lord

*Acting Assistant Surgeon J. M. De Wolf

Acting Assistant Surgeon Henry R. Porter

Company

A Capt. Myles Moylan; 1st Lt. Charles C. DeRudio; 2d Lt. Charles A. Varnum (detached to command Indian scouts).

B Capt. Thomas M. McDougall; *2d Lt. Benjamin H. Hodgson (detached as adjutant to Major Reno).

C *Capt. Thomas W. Custer; *2d Lt. Henry M. Harrington.

D Capt. Thomas B. Weir; 2d Lt.Winfield S. Edgerly.

E *1st Lt. Algernon E. Smith; *2d Lt. James G. Sturgis.

F *Capt. George W. Yates; *2d Lt. William Van W. Reily.

G *1st Lt. Donald McIntosh; 2d Lt. George D.Wallace.

H Capt. Frederick W. Benteen; 1st Lt. Francis M. Gibson.

I *Capt. Myles W. Keogh; *2d Lt. James E. Porter.

K 1st Lt. Edward S. Godfrey; 2d Lt. Luther R. Hare (detached with Indian scouts).

L *1st Lt. James Calhoun; *2d Lt. John J. Crittenden (20th Infantry attached to 7th Calvary temporarily).

M Capt. Thomas H. French; 1st Lt. Edward G. Mathey (detached to command packtrain).

Civilians

*Boston Custer, brother of General Custer

*Harry Armstrong Reed, nephew of General Custer

*Mark Kellogg, reporter for Bismarck *Tribune*

*Frank C. Mann, chief packer

*Charley Reynolds, chief scout

*Isaiah Dorman, Negro, Indian interpreter

*Mitch Bouyer, mixed-blood scout

Fred Gerard, interpreter

II. Low Dog's Account of the Battle of the Little Bighorn

In July 1881 reporters interviewed the Oglala Sioux Chief Low Dog at Standing Rock Agency, Dakota Territory. This is the account, as published in the *Leavenworth* (Kan.) *Weekly Times* of August 18, 1881:

We were in camp near Little Big Horn river. We had lost some horses, and an Indian went back on the trail to look for them. We did not know that the white warriors were coming after us. Some scouts or men in advance of the warriors saw the Indian looking for the horses and ran after him and tried to kill him to keep him from bringing us word, but he ran faster than they and came into camp and told us that the white warriors were coming. I was asleep in my lodge at the time. The sun was about noon (pointing with his finger). I heard the alarm, but I did not believe it. I thought it was a false alarm. I did not think it possible that any white men would attack us, so strong as we were. We had in camp the Cheyennes, Arapahoes, and seven different tribes of the Teton Sioux—a countless number. Although I did not believe it was a true alarm, I lost no time getting ready. When I got my gun and came out of my lodge the attack had begun at the end of the camp where Sitting Bull and the Uncpapas were. The Indians held their ground to give the women and children time to get out of the way. By this time the herders were driving in the horses and as I was nearly at the further end of the camp, I ordered my men to catch their horses and get out of the way, and my men were hurrying to go and help those that were fighting. When the fighters saw that the women and children were safe they fell back. By this time my people went to help them, and the less able warriors and the women caught horses and got them ready, and we drove the first attacking party back, and that party retreated to a high hill. Then I told my people not to venture too far in pursuit for fear of falling into an ambush. By this time all the warriors in our camp were mounted and ready for fight, and then we were attacked on the other side by another party. They came on us like a thunderbolt. I never before nor since saw men so brave and fearless as those white warriors. We retreated until our men got all together, and then we charged upon them. I called to my men, "This is a good day to die: follow me." We massed our men, and that no man should fall back, every man whipped another man's horse and we rushed right upon them. As we rushed upon them the white warriors dismounted to fire, but they did very poor shooting. They held their horses reins on one arm while they were shoot-ing, but their horses were so frightened that they pulled the men all around, and a great many of their shots went up in the air and did us no harm. The white warriors stood their ground bravely, and none of them made any attempt to get away. After all but two of them were killed, I captured two of their horses. Then the wise men and chiefs of our nation gave out to our people not to mutilate the dead white chief, for he was a brave warrior and died a brave man, and his remains should be respected.

Then I turned around and went to help fight the other white warriors, who had retreated to a high hill on the east side of the river.... I don't know whether any white men of Custer's force were taken prisoners. When I got back to our camp they were all dead. Everything was in confusion all the time of the fight. I did not see Gen. Custer. I do not know who killed him. We did not know till the fight was over that he was the white chief. We had no idea that the white warriors were coming until the runner came in and told us. I do not say that Reno was a coward. He fought well, but our men were fighting to save their women and children, and drive them back. If Reno and his warriors had fought as Custer and his warriors fought, the battle might have been against us. No white man or Indian ever fought as bravely as Custer and his men. The next day we fought Reno and his forces again, and killed many of them. Then the chiefs said these men had been punished enough, and that we ought to be merciful, and let them go. Then we heard that another force was coming up the river to fight us . . . and we started to fight them, but the chiefs and wise men counseled that we had fought enough and that we should not fight unless attacked, and we went back and took our women and children and went away.

This ended Low Dog's narration, given in the hearing of half a dozen officers, some of the Seventeenth Infantry and some of the Seventh Cavalry—Custer's regiment. It was in the evening; the sun had set and the twilight was deepening. Officers were there who were at the Big Horn with Benteen, senior captain of the Seventh, who usually exercised command as a field officer, and who, with his battalion, joined Reno on the first day of the fight, after his retreat, and was in the second day's fight. It was a strange and intensely interesting scene. When Low Dog began his narrative only Capt. Howe, the interpreter, and myself were present, but as he progressed the officers gathered round, listening to every word, and all were impressed that the Indian chief was giving a true account, according to his knowledge. Some one asked how many Indians were killed in the fight, Low Dog answered, "Thirty-eight, who died then, and a great many—I can't tell the number —who were wounded and died afterwards. I never saw a fight in which so many in proportion to the killed were wounded, and so many horses were wounded." Another asked who were the dead Indians that were found in two tepees—five in one and six in the other—all richly dressed, and with their ponies, slain about the tepees. He said eight were chiefs killed in the battle. One was his own brother, born of the same mother and the same father, and he did not know who the other two were.

The question was asked, "What part did Sitting Bull take in the fight?" Low Dog is not friendly to Sitting Bull. He answered with a sneer: "If some one would lend him a heart he would fight." Then Low Dog said he would like to go home, and with the interpreter he went back to the Indian camp. He is a tall, straight Indian, thirty-four years old, not a bad face, regular features and small hands and feet. He said that when he had his weapons and was on the war-path he considered no man his superior; but when he surrendered he laid that feeling all aside, and now if any man should try to chastise him in his humble condition and helplessness all he could do would be to tell him that he was no man and a coward; which, while he was on the war-path he would allow no man to say and live.

He said that when he was fourteen years old, he had his first experience on the war-path: "I went against the will of my parents and those having authority over me. It was on a stream above the mouth of the Yellowstone. We went to war against a band of Assiniboins that were hunting buffalo, and I killed one of their men. After we killed all of that band another band came out against us, and I killed one of them. When we came back to our tribe I was made a chief, as no Sioux had ever been known to kill two enemies in one fight at my age, and I was invited into the councils of the chiefs and wise men. At that time we had no thought that we would ever fight the whites. Then I heard some people talking that the chief of the white men wanted the Indians to live where he ordered and do as he said, and he would feed and clothe them. I was called into council with the chiefs and wise men, and we had a talk about that. My judgment was why should I allow any man to support me against my will anywhere, so long as I have hands and as long as I am an able man, not a boy. Little I thought then that I would have to fight the white man, or do as he should tell me. When it began to be plain that we would have to yield or fight, we had a great many councils. I said, why should I be kept as an humble man, when I am a brave warrior and on my own lands? The game is mine, and the hills, and the valleys, and the white man has no right to say where I shall go or what I shall do. If any white man tries to destroy my property, or take my lands, I will take my gun, get on my horse, and go punish him. I never thought that I would have to change that view. But at last I saw that if I wished to do good to my nation, I would have to do it by wise thinking and not so much fighting. Now, I want to learn the white man's way, for I see that he is stronger than we are, and that his government is better than ours."

III. Gall's account of The Battle of the Little Bighorn

One of the principal Sioux leaders, the Hunkpapa Chief Gall, attended the 10th anniversary observance at Custer Battlefield in June 1886. An interview with him on the scene of Custer's annihilation was published as follows in the *St. Paul* (Minn.) *Pioneer Press* of July 18, 1886:

"How long before all the soldiers were killed?" The chief made the sign of the white man's dinner time which means noon, and then with his finger cut a half, which would signify half an hour consumed in slaughtering everybody.

"Did the red men shoot guns or arrows?"

"Both. We soon shot all our cartridges, and then shot arrows and used our war clubs."

"Did the soldiers have plenty of ammunition?"

"No. They shot away all they had. The horses ran away, carrying in the saddle pockets a heap more. The soldiers threw their guns aside and fought with little guns." (Pistols.)

"Who got the horses?"

"The Cheyenne women. A lot of horses got into the river and I jumped in and caught them."

The chief's mind seemed to dwell particularly upon the number of horses they captured rather than the terrible slaughter which took place.

"Did the Indians fight standing up?"

"No. The soldiers did, but the braves fired from behind their horses. A lot of Indians fell over and died."

"When the soldiers had no more cartridges left what did the Indians do?"

"The braves ran up to the soldiers and killed them with hatchets."

"How many Indians were killed?"

"Eleven down in that creek, four over there and two in that coulee."

"How many were killed, altogether?"

"Forty-three in all. A great many crossed the river and died in the rushes. They died every day. Nearly as many died each day as were killed in the fight. We buried them in trees and on scaffolds going up Lodge Pole Creek toward the White Rain mountains."

"How many different tribes were in the fight?"

"Uncpapa, Minneconjou, Ogalalla, Brule, Teton, Santee and Yanktonnais Sioux, Blackfeet, Cheyennes, Arapahoes, and a few Gros Ventres."

"Who fought first, Custer or Reno?"

"Reno was whipped first and then all with Custer were killed."

Of course the chief did not understand the names Custer and Reno, but he indicated by pointing and other signs whom he meant.

"How soon after Reno charged did Custer come down the valley?"

"We saw all at one time before they separated. When Reno charged, the women and children were moved down stream: and when the Sioux bucks drove Reno on top of the bluffs, everybody came down and fought Custer. All the Indians were mixed up then."

"How soon after Reno charged was Custer attacked?"

No satisfactory answer could be gotten to this important question; but it would seem that as soon as Reno was lodged safely on the hill the whole village massed on Custer at once and annihilated him.

"Did Custer get near the river?"

"No."

"Then how came the dead bodies of soldiers on the river's bank where we think the white chief crossed or attempted to cross?"

Gall's answer came without a moment's hesitation.

"They were soldiers who fled down another coulee, crossed the river lower down, were chased up stream again toward the village, driven back into the river, and killed on this side."

"Did the soldiers fight on horseback or on foot?"

"They fought on foot. One man held the horses while the others shot the guns. We tried to kill the holders, and then by waving blankets and shouting we scared the horses down that coulee, where the Cheyenne women caught them."

"Did you kill any soldiers?"

" Yes, I killed a great many. I killed them all with the hatchet; I did not use a gun."

"Who had command of all the red men?"

"I held command of those down stream."

"Who was the first one killed with Reno?"

"I don't know; but some of the Sioux say it was a Crow [Arikara] scout named Bloody Knife."

"Where was Sitting Bull all this time while the white soldiers were being killed?"

"Back in his tepee making medicine."

"Did he fight at all?"

"No; he made medicine for us."

"Did you fight Reno?"

"No; I only fought the white men soldiers down this way."

"Then you know nothing of what happened at the upper end of the village?"

"No, I was down among the Cheyennes looking after horses when the first attack was made on our village."

"Did the old men and boys fight too?"

" Yes, and the squaws fought with stone clubs and hatchet knives. The squaws cut off the boot legs."

"Were there any white men or breeds in your camp?"

"No; we had only Indians."

"Did the soldiers have swords?"

"No, there was only one long knife with them, and he was killed too."

"Who had the long knife?"

"I don't know."

"Did you see Curley on that day?" (Pointing out the Crow scout who is the only survivor of all who marched with Custer into the Little Big Horn valley.)

"No; but my braves say he ran away early and did not fight at all."

"Did you take any prisoners, and if so what did you do with them?"

This question was put to find out if possible the true fate of Lieutenants Harrington, Jack Sturgis, Dr. Lord, and about fourteen others whose bodies were not found on the field, nor has anything been heard of them since the morning when the command was divided.

"No, we took no prisoners. Our hearts were bad, and we cut and shot them all to pieces."

"Do you remember seeing Custer, the big chief, after the fight?"

"I saw the big chief riding with the orderly before we attacked. He had glasses to his face (field glasses). During the fight there were too many soldiers scattered all around for me to see him."

"Did any of the soldiers get away?"

"No, all were killed. About fourteen (indicating the number with his fingers) started toward the Wolf Mountains, but the young braves got on their trail and all were killed."

No doubt Harrington, Sturgis, Lord and the other missing ones were of this party endeavoring to escape toward the Wolf Mountains.

"What did you do after all Custer's soldiers were killed?"

"We went back to fight the soldiers on the hill who were digging holes in the ground. We staid there until big dust was seen down the river, when we all moved up Lodge Pole Creek toward the White Rain Mountains."

IV. A Participant's Account of Major Reno's Battle

One of the more literate members of Major Reno's battalion was John M. Ryan, first sergeant of Capt. Thomas H. French's Company M. This extract from his recollections appeared in the *Hardin* (Mont.) *Tribune*, June 22, 1923:

Reno's battalion started down the valley, first on a trot, and then at a gallop, marching in columns of twos. Lieutenant Varnum, a very brave young officer in command of the scouts, rode ahead of Reno's battalion. He swung his hat around in the air, and sung out to the men, "Thirty days' furlough to the man who gets the first scalp." We were very anxious for the furlough, but not so particular about the scalp.

We arrived at the bank of the Little Big Horn river and waded to the other side, and here there was a very strong current, and there was quicksand about three feet deep. On the other side of the river we made a short halt, dismounted, tightened our saddle girths, and then swung into our saddles. After mounting we came up, "Left front into line," Captain French's Company M on the right and Lieutenant Mc-Intosh's company on the left, and Captain Moylan's in the rear.

We were then in the valley of the Little Big Horn, and facing down stream. We started down on a trot and then on a slow gallop. Between the right of my company and the river bank there was quite a lot of underbrush, and bullberry bushes. Captain French gave me orders to take 10 men off to the right of my company and form a skirmish line, so as to cover the brush from the right of our line to the river bank, as the Indians might be lurking there. We advanced in that formation from one and a half to two miles, until we came to a heavy piece of timber.

Hears First Shot

Before we arrived at the timber, there was one shot fired away ahead of us. I did not know whether it was fired by Lieutenant Varnum's scouts or one of the hostile Indians. That was the first shot that I heard in the opening of the battle of the Little Big Horn on June 25, 1876, and I had pretty good ears about that time.

Private James Turley of my troop when we arrived at the timber and had orders to halt, could not control his horse which carried him towards the Indian camp. That was the last I saw of him. He was a very nice young man. A little incident happened a day or two before we left Fort Rice to go on the expedition. Turley asked me if I would allow him to put some of his property in my clothes chest. I told him that I would with the understanding that if he was killed the contents of the chest would belong to me and if I was killed it would belong to him. After coming back from the expedition the property belonging to those men that were killed was sold at public auction and the proceeds turned over to the paymaster.

When we got to the timber we rode down an embankment and dismounted. This was where the channel of the river changed and was probably several feet lower than the level of the prairie. We dismounted in haste, number four of each set of four holding the horses.

We came up onto higher ground forming a skirmish line from the timber towards the bluffs on the other side of the valley and facing down stream in the direction of the Indian camp. This was our first view of the Indian camp from the skirmish line. Some of the men laid down while others knelt down.

At this particular place there was a prairiedog town and we used the mounds for temporary breast works. We got the skirmish line formed and here the Indians made their first charge. There were probably 500 of them coming from the direction of their village. They were well mounted and well armed. They tried to cut through our skirmish line. We fired volleys into them repulsing their charge and emptying a number of their saddles.

Lieutenant Hodgson walked up and down the line encouraging the men to keep cool and fire low.

First Man Killed

Finally when they could not cut through us, they strung out in a single file, lying on the opposite side of their ponies from us, and then they commenced to circle. They overlapped our skirmish line on the left and were closing in on the rear to complete the circle. We had orders to fall back to our horses. This was where the first man was killed, Sergt. Miles F. O'Hara of my troop M. He was a corporal going out on the expedition and promoted to a sergeant a few days before his death to replace Sergt. John Dolan, who was discharged, as his term of service had expired, and was back with the wagon trains at Powder river. Sergeant O'Hara was considered a very fine soldier in M troop and we missed him very much.

In the Indian camp after the battle, when we were destroying it, we found the heads of three of our men tied together with wires and suspended from a lodge pole with their hair all burned off. We did not see their bodies there. The Indians probably threw them into the river. We got back to our horses and the orders were given to mount and this time some of the men became confused and some of them could not find their horses.

Major Reno had lost his hat and had a red handkerchief tied around his head. As we mounted I looked to the rear in the direction of the river and saw the Indians completing the circle, riding through the brush and lying flat on their ponies. I mentioned the fact to Captain French, saying: "Captain, the Indians are in our rear." He answered: "Oh, no; those are General Custer's men." Just at that moment one of those Indians fired and Private George Lorentz of my company, who was number one of the first set of fours, was shot, the bullet striking him in the back of his neck and coming out of his mouth. He fell forward on his saddle and dropped to the ground.

Just at that moment the Indians fired into us from all sides, and I said to Captain French of my company: "The best thing that we can do is to cut right through them." By this time they had us surrounded. They were on higher ground than we were. Major Reno rode up and said: "Any of you men who wish to make your escape, follow me."

Reno Leads Charge

The order was then given to charge, and away we went up the steep embankment, cutting through the Indians in a solid body, Major Reno being in advance. As we cut through them the fighting was hand to hand, and it was death to any man who fell from his horse, or was wounded and was not able to keep up with the command.

After cutting through we went back over the same ground, and took a circle to the left to gain the bluffs at the nearest point. Here there was some pretty sharp fighting. The Indians were in great numbers on all sides of us. In this charge there were 30 men killed, my company losing 10, but we reached the river.

Bloody Knife, chief of Indian scouts; Charlie Reynolds, a white scout, and Izar Dorman, the negro interpreter, were killed here. Lieutenant Hodgson was wounded, and had his horse shot, and Lieut. Donald McIntosh was killed. McIntosh was a brave and faithful officer, commanding Company G.

Lieutenant DeRudio and Fred Girard, a white scout, and some 10 or 12 men became separated from the command and hid themselves in the brush or in the woods, or under the river embankment, and some of those men told me afterwards that they stood in water up to their necks, under the embankment, to keep out of sight of the Indians. Two of those men were sergeants of my company, Charles White and Patrick Carney. They joined the command in the intrenchments on the bluff, after dark.

At this point the river was about 50 yards wide, and the water about two and a half feet deep, with a swift current. Lieutenant Hodgson asked one of the men to carry him across, he being wounded and his horse being shot. It was reported that a trumpeter from my company named Fisher, better known as "Bounce," told him to hold on to his stirrup, and the horse drew the lieutenant as well as the rider across the river. He was shot a second time and killed. Now I know of three men who claim to have aided Hodgson.

Fighting is Desperate

The opposite bank of the river was very steep, and the only way to get up to the bluffs was through a buffalo trail worn on the bank, and only wide enough to let one man pass through at a time. Before we crossed the river the fighting was desperate and at close quarters.

In many instances the soldiers would empty their revolvers right into the breasts of the Indians, and after these were empty some were seen to throw them away, and grab their carbines, not having time to return their revolvers to their holsters. In my opinion, if Reno had remained in the timber a short time longer not a man would have made his escape as the Indians outnumbered us 10 to one.

In scaling the bluff, Dr. DeWolf, a contract surgeon on the expedition, was killed; also Sergeant Clair of Company K, William D. Myer, a farrier of company M, and Henry Gordon of the same company. Their bodies, with a number of others, lay under cover of our guns, so that the Indians did not get a chance to scalp them.

After we gained the bluffs we could look back upon the plains where the Indians were, and could see them stripping and scalping our men, and mutilating their bodies in a horrible manner. The prairie was all afire. The officers did all in their power to rally the men, and while they were doing so many were killed.

After the companies were formed the firing ceased, and we were joined by Benteen's battalion, which was the first we had seen of him since the division of the regiment. Soon after, the pack train arrived, with Company B, under Captain McDougall, which was very fortunate, as our ammunition was nearly exhausted, and we could not get supplies from any other source. We had several wounded men and we attended to them as well as circumstances would permit. I understood at that time that Captain Weir with his company D, left the command there, and started in the direction General Custer took for a short distance, and then returned, although I did not see him.

Leaving two companies with the packs and wounded, Major Reno, with five companies, or what was left of them, proceeded in the direction we had supposed General Custer took, and in the direction of the Indian camp.

We went in that direction for probably half a mile until we gained a high point and could overlook the Indian camp and the battlefield. We saw at a distance of from a mile and a half to two miles parties whom we supposed were Indians, riding back and forth, firing scattering shots. We thought that they were disposing of Custer's wounded men, and this afterward proved to be true.

We halted for a few moments, and saw a large herd of ponies at the further end of the village, and could distinguish a large party of Indians coming towards the Indian camp. The prairie around the village and the first battlefield was all afire, having been set by the Indians to hide their movements.

At the top of this bluff we halted, and at foot there was a ford, and this was where Custer had first encountered the Indians, as we found some of the dead bodies there two days afterwards. While we were on the bluffs the Indians again made their appearance, coming in large numbers from the direction in which we heard the firing. We exchanged several shots with them, and we lost a few men, and then had orders to fall back to our packs and wounded.

On our arriving there we dismounted in haste, putting the wounded in a low depression on the bluffs and put packs from the mules around them to shelter them from the fire of the Indians. We then formed a circle of our pack mules and horses, forming a skirmish line all around the hole, and then lay down and waited for the Indians.

Indians Surround Them

We had been in this position but a short time when they advanced in great numbers from the direction in which we came.

They made several charges upon us and we repulsed them every time. Finally they surrounded us. Soon the firing became general all along the line, very rapid and at close range. The company on the right of my company had a number of men killed in a few minutes. There was a high ridge on the right and an opening on the right of our lines, and one Indian in particular I must give credit for being a good shot.

While we were lying in this line he fired a shot and killed the fourth man on my right. Soon afterward he fired again and shot the third man. His third shot wounded the man on my right, who jumped back from the line, and down among the rest of the wounded. I thought my turn was coming next. I jumped up, with Captain French, and some half a dozen members of my company, and, instead of firing straight to the front, as we had been doing up to the time of this incident, we wheeled to our right and put in a deadly volley, and I think we put an end to that Indian, as there were no more men killed at that particular spot.

Captain French was as brave an officer as ever served in the Seventh Cavalry, and was known to have killed several Indians on different occasions. He had a Springfield rifle, caliber .50, breechloader, and it was his custom, whenever he shot an Indian, to cut a notch in the stock of that gun.

I remember on one occasion he fired at a curlew, two or three shots, and did not hit it. He felt so discouraged that he took the gun and threw it away. A little later I picked it up and rolled it up in a blanket, put it in one of the government wagons, and brought it into Fort Rice, Dakota, after the expedition broke up, unknown to him, and when he learned that I had it he reclaimed it. He retired from the service some years afterwards, and I have been informed, I am sorry to say, he met with a fatal accident.

When dark set in, it closed the engagement on the twenty-fifth. We went to work with what tools we had, consisting of two spades, our knives and tin cups, and, in fact, we used pieces of hard tack boxes for spades, and commenced throwing up temporary works. We also formed breastworks from boxes of hard bread, sacks of bacon, sacks of corn and oats, blankets, and in fact everything that we could get hold of.

During the night ammunition and the rations reached us where we were entrenched in the lines, but we suffered severely from lack of water. Although the river was only three or four hundred yards away, we were unable to get any water, as the Indians held the approach to it. During the night several men made attempts to get water, but they were killed or driven back.

About the middle of the night we heard a trumpet call, and the men commenced to cheer, thinking it was Custer's men who were coming to our assistance. Major Reno ordered one of our trumpeters to sound a call, but it was not repeated, so we made up our minds that it was a decoy on the part of the Indians to get us out of our works.

Benteen Hard Pressed

The trumpet that they used probably belonged to one of Custer's trumpeters, but we did not know it at that time. We had no thought of leaving our works, as we had a number of our men wounded there, and some of them pretty badly.

At intervals during the night we could hear the Indians riding back and forth across the river. I have an idea that they thought we were going to make a rush and get out of there.

The next morning, being the 26th, two shots were fired just before daylight by the Indians, in rapid succession. All this time we were wondering what had become of Custer and his troops. This began the engagement of another day. In a few moments the battle raged in earnest, the Indians advancing in large numbers and trying to cut through.

Captain Benteen's company particularly was hard pressed, and the men did their utmost to repulse those Indians who were gaining ground on the troops. Captain Benteen called out to Major Reno for re-enforcements, saying: "The Indians are doing their best to cut through my lines, and it will be impossible for me to hold my position much longer." Captain French's Company M was immediately withdrawn from that part of the line which they occupied, and rushed to the assistance of Captain Benteen's company. Both companies made a charge on the Indians and drove them down the hill, but in doing so we lost a number of men. This section of the battlefield was a little higher than the balance of the ground.

Private Tanner Killed

Had the Indians been successful, the day would have been lost, and Reno's command would have shared the fate of Custer's brave men, as Captain Benteen said afterward.

Private James Tanner of Company M, was badly wounded in this charge, and his body lay on the side of the bluffs in an exposed position. There was a call for volunteers to bring him down, and I grabbed a blanket with three other men, rushed to his assistance, rolled him into the blanket, and made quick tracks in getting him from the side of the bluffs to where our wounded lay. Fortunately none of the rescuing party received anything more than a few balls through their clothing. After placing Tanner with the rest of the wounded, he died in a few minutes.

There was a gray horse belonging to my company, that was ridden by Captain French, and he was the best buffalo horse in the command. He was among the other horses near the wounded, and an Indian shot him through the head. He was staggering about among the other horses, and Private Henry C. Voyt, of my company took hold of him to lead him out of the way of the other horses, and Voyt at the same instant had his brains blown out. We buried Private Tanner, about whom I have made some explanation, and Voyt in the same grave the next morning. Then we made a head board out of a piece of hardtack box, and marked their names with a lead pencil on the board, and drove it into the ground.

Indian Fire Slackens

Late in the day the fire of the Indians slackened, except on the point of a high bluff in the direction in which it was supposed that Custer had gone. Here the Indians put in a few well-directed shots that laid several of our men low. I do not know what kind of a gun one of those Indians used, but it made a tremendous noise, and, in fact those Indians were out of range of our carbine, which were Springfields, caliber .45.

Captain French of my company asked me if I could do anything with those Indians, as they were out of range of the carbines. I told the captain that I would try, and as I was the owner of a 15-pound Sharp's telescope rifle, caliber .45, which I had had made in Bismarck before the expedition started out, and which cost me $100. I fired a couple of shots until I got range of that group of Indians. Then I put in half a dozen shots in rapid succession, and those Indians scampered away from that point of the bluff, and that ended the firing on the part of the Indians in that memorable engagement, and the boys set up quite a cheer.

The Indians all scampered from the bluffs across the river and moved back to their encampment. We could see them pulling down their lodges and getting ready for a hasty removal. In a short time they stripped the hides off their lodges and left the poles standing and moved out from their camp up the valley of the Little Big Horn, and over the field where Major Reno's battalion fought in the beginning of the engagement, and where his dead lay. It was the largest body of Indians that I ever saw move together at one time.

I have seen the Cheyennes, the Arapahoes, the Kiowas, the Apaches, and the Comanches move together in the Indian territory, and in Kansas years before, while campaigning there under General Custer, I should say that there were double the number moving out from this camp.

When they moved, the captain of my company, Thomas H. French, and I fired into them while they remained in range of our two guns, and those were the last shots fired in the battle of the Little Big Horn. That was well known by every man in Reno's battalion.

Major Reno, Captain French, Captain Benteen, Captain McDougall, Captain Weir, Lieutenant Godfrey and, in fact all of the officers did all that they could in order to defeat the Indians, and some of the officers must have had a charmed life the way they stood up under this heavy fire.

I think the Indians took some of our men prisoners, and when other reinforcements joined us we found what appeared to be human bones, and parts of blue uniforms, where the men had been tied to stakes and trees. Some of the bodies of our officers were not found, at least not at that time. Among them were Lieutenants Harrington, Porter and Sturgis. I understood that some parts of their clothing, uniform or gauntlet gloves were found on the field, which showed that they were killed. In burying the dead many of the bodies were not identified.

After the Indians moved out of sight we jumped out of our works, built better rifles pits, and unsaddled our horses, which had not been unsaddled since the evening of the twenty-fourth.

45 Men Killed

We also took the packs from the mules. Then we got water from the river in camp kettles, and made a better shelter for the horses and wounded, for we expected that the Indians would attack us again.

Reno's command lost, between the engagement in the bottom and the entrenchments on the bluffs, somewhere about 45 men killed and 60 wounded, which will show how desperate the engagement was. In my company, out of 45 men and horses that went into the engagement, 14 men and the second lieutenant were killed, 10 wounded, and we lost about 15 horses killed or disabled.

That night everything was quiet as far as the Indians were concerned. The next morning at daylight we could look from the bluffs over the timber to where the Indian camp was, and we saw that it was deserted, with the exception of the lodge poles, which remained standing. On the other side, a long way off from the Indian camp, we noticed a large cloud of dust arising, and a body of either Indians or troops coming towards the Indian camp, but at the time we could not distinguish which they were.

Some of the officers turned their field glasses on, and thought they were troops. Reno immediately dispatched a couple of his scouts, and it proved to be the balance of our expedition, and General Gibbon's command under General Alfred Terry. It appears that they came through Custer's battlefield, and they counted the dead bodies of 207 men. They then crossed the river.

CUSTER'S LAST CAMPAIGN
A PHOTOGRAPHIC ESSAY

George Armstrong Custer once boasted that his 7th Cavalry alone could whip all the Indians on the Plains. While this might be dismissed as a pardonable exaggeration, the 7th did enjoy a reputation as the most experienced and capable mounted regiment in the U.S. Army. It guarded emigrants and freighters, mail stages, and telegraph lines. It undertook explorations into little-known regions, and it protected scientific expeditions into new territory. Sometimes it evicted white trespassers from Indian reservations, and sometimes it fought in bloody campaigns against the Indians. Because the exploits of the 7th and its flamboyant leader drew considerable public attention, newspaper correspondents and commercial photographers sometimes accompanied the regiment on tours of duty to record its activities.

When Custer and the 7th marched out of Fort Lincoln in mid-May 1876, however, no photographer rode with them. The campaign was to be a fast, hard-hitting drive against the recalcitrant Sioux and Cheyenne, and there was no place for the slow and cumbersome equipment needed by photographers of the day. As a result, there is no photographic record of the campaign and battle that brought disaster to Custer and the 7th on the banks of the Little Bighorn 1 month later.

The record that does remain, however, is nonetheless impressive. It consists of photographs taken before and after the campaign, which, ranging from the neat and orderly Fort Lincoln to the debris-littered fields of the Little Bighorn, provide a striking contrast that serves to deepen the sense of the tragedy. The following photographs, with their captions, highlight salient portions of the main narrative; but, they also form a capsule history of the campaign that proved to be Custer's last.

Fort Abraham Lincoln, Dakota Territory. Located on the west bank of the Missouri River about 10 miles south of Bismarck, the territorial capital, Fort Lincoln was Custer's base of operations from 1873

until 1876. It was from here on May 17, 1876, that the Dakota Column set out on the campaign that ended in Custer's defeat and death on the Little Bighorn.

Group of 7th Cavalry officers and ladies at Fort Lincoln shortly before the regiment left on the Little Bighorn campaign. General Custer is third from the left; Mrs. Custer is the first lady from the left on the lower step.

Custer and his wife in their home at Fort Lincoln, about 1875. Large portrait on the wall at left is of Custer in Civil War garb; the one on the right is of Gen. Philip Sheridan.

Col. John Gibbon led the Montana Column on the march from Fort Ellis to the Little Bighorn. A battle-scarred veteran of 34 years service, Gibbon gained fame in the Civil War as commander of the "Iron Brigade," and later rose to the rank of major general and the command of an infantry corps. After the war he continued in the Regular Army, serving for nearly 20 years as colonel of the 7th Infantry.

Brig. Gen. Alfred H. Terry commanded the Dakota Column. A former lawyer, he rose to the rank of major general in the Civil War and distinguished himself in the capture of Fort Fisher, S.C. Near the end of the war he secured a brigadier's commission in the Regular Army and was later assigned to command the Department of Dakota. Although not a professional soldier, Terry proved an able and well–liked general.

Gatling guns, like these at Fort Lincoln, accompanied the Dakota Column. General Terry offered them to Custer, who could have used them to advantage during the battle. Getting them there, however,

would have been a difficult task, and most historians agree that Custer was right in declining to accept the delays they would have imposed on his march.

Capt. Thomas B. Weir, D Company commander, led the abortive attempt to break through to Custer's relief.

Lt. Charles A. Varnum had charge of Custer's Indian scouts. He died in 1934, the last surviving officer of Reno's command.

Capt. Thomas W. Custer, holder of two Congressional Medals of Honor, fell with the "last stand" group near his older brother.

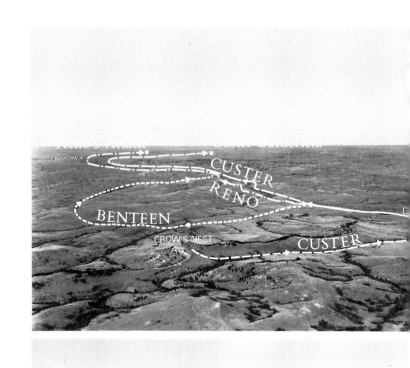

Custer viewed the distant Little Bighorn Valley from the Crow's Nest at dawn on June 25. At noon the regiment paused on the divide between the Rosebud and Little Bighorn watershed, while Custer formed three battalions for the advance on the enemy, whose exact location was not yet known.

Reno crossed the Little Bighorn and charged the upper end of the Indian camp, but was thrown back across the river. On Reno Hill he united with Captain Benteen and later the pack train. Custer, meanwhile, had vanished downstream.

After scanning the valley from the bluff just north of Reno Hill, Custer led his battalion down a deep ravine to Medicine Tail Coulee, across to Deep Coulee, and up to the battle ridge. Here his command

Last Stand

CONJECTURAL ROUTE

Martini Sent Back

CUSTER

was wiped out by warriors pouring across the river from the village. Captain Weir tried to come to his aid, but was forced to turn back by Indians who met him at Weir Point.

Custer's last message is now preserved in the library of the U.S. Military Academy at West Point, N.Y. At the top is Benteen's "translation" of Adjutant Cooke's hastily scrawled summons.

Lt. William W. Cooke, a Canadian soldier of fortune, was the 7th Cavalry's able adjutant. He scribbled the message on a page torn from his memorandum book, and died an hour later on Custer Hill.

Sgt. John Martin at the time of his retirement in 1904. As Giovanni Martini, he was detailed as Custer's orderly on June 25, 1876, and carried the last message through Sioux warriors to Benteen.

Captain Keogh's claybank gelding, Comanche, was the only survivor of the battle for the U.S. Army. Near death with arrow and bullet wounds, the horse was found on the battlefield on June 27 and,

with Reno's wounded soldiers, was taken aboard the steamer Far West *for the journey back to Fort Lincoln. Comanche's remains are now enshrined at the University of Kansas.*

In the summer of 1877, one year after the battle, Captain Keogh's reconstituted Company I returned to the battlefield to reclaim the bodies of the officers and rebury those of the enlisted men. Keogh's marker stands on the spot where he fell.

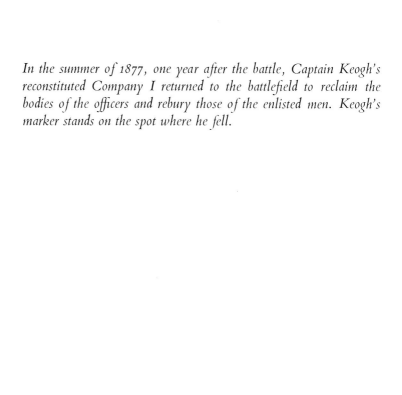

Horse bones still littered the field when Company I returned. The wooden stakes mark the graves of the slain.

83

Custer's Crow scouts visit Custer Battlefield about 1916. Left to

right: White-Man-Runs-Him, Hairy Moccasin, Curley, Goes Ahead.

Sioux warriors typical of those who fought Custer

photographed at Standing Rock Agency in 1879.

The blue-and-gold regimental standard of the 7th Cavalry remained with the pack train during the battle.

Each company carried a stars and stripes guidon. This one is similar to those carried in the battle.

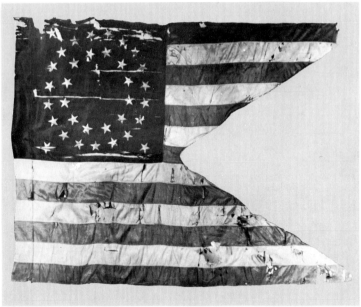

Chartered by the Government for the campaign of 1876, the Far West *performed important service in transporting troops, supplies, and dispatches. With Reno's wounded on board, the boat steamed from the mouth of the Bighorn to Bismarck, 710 miles, in 54 hours—a record unsurpassed in steamboating on the Upper Missouri.*

On October 10, 1877, the remains of Bvt. Maj. Gen. George Armstrong Custer, lieutenant colonel of the 7th Cavalry, were buried with full military honors in the cemetery near the Old Cadet Chapel at the U.S. Military Academy, West Point, N.Y. Today, a large granite monument marks the grave.

THE ART AND THE ARTIST

Leonard Baskin, sculptor, draftsman, printer, and printmaker, is the latest in a seemingly infinite series of artists who have portrayed the events of June 25, 1876. The decision to commission the drawings reproduced in this handbook is a most proper service to the memory of the Battle of the Little Bighorn. Baskin cuts through a century of mediocre, apocryphal pictures to reveal the actors of this tragic drama as they were, not in the event, but in life and in death.

In 1968 an effort was made by the staff of the Amon Carter Museum in Fort Worth to catalogue the many pictures of the Custer fight. With more than 900 versions identified, it is an established fact that this sad occasion is the most memorialized single event in American history. A deluge of paintings, prints, sculptures, cigarette cards, bottle caps, whiskey labels—not to mention murals—have been inspired by the battle. Each, of course, is the product of the artist's imagination. Many have been copied even three and four times, while others are sincere efforts at historical reconstruction of the event based upon documents, eye-witness accounts, and physical remains.

In a situation where imagination may properly replace truth (no witness survived to contest the artist), it is curious that almost every artist to the present time has been absorbed in the reality of the event and has neglected the human overtones—the sullen quiet of the Indian betrayed—the sudden surprise and totality of death on the vast plains—the frustration of hindsight judgments—the responsibilities and loyalties obliterated in the aftermath. There were no victors that day; just survivors, each aware that a day of reckoning had passed and another would soon be upon them. As in any disaster, many people learn much, but too late.

If this foreboding air hangs over Baskin's drawings to leave the reader disquieted, it is because the artist has sensed the real tragedy of Custer and the Indians. Authority and manifest destiny had in some way contradicted our "solemn word" and treaty obligations. Custer and his men became the instruments to correct a situation embarrassing both in Washington and on the frontier—a change of mind. Examine Baskin's drawings—Indians and officers; all are asking "Why?"

We see man's mortality, brutality, and futility. And yet we read in the faces of Baskin's people the basic humanity which ties us together in a tragic climax no one seems to comprehend.

Leonard Baskin teaches art at Smith College, Northampton, Mass. His work is represented in collections of the major art museums of the United States by examples of sculpture, drawings, prints, and fine press books. His genius, combined with a great sense of design and typography, is reflected in the publications of the Gehenna Press, founded by Baskin in 1942 and now located at Northampton.

Mitchell A. Wilder November 1968

ADMINISTRATION

Custer Battlefield National Monument is administered by the National Park Service, U.S. Department of the Interior. A superintendent, whose address is Crow Agency, Mont. 59022, is in immediate charge.

As the Nation's principal conservation agency, the Department of the Interior has basic responsibilities for water, fish, wildlife, mineral, land, park, and recreational resources. Indian and Territorial affairs are other major concerns of America's "Department of Natural Resources." The Department works to assure the wisest choice in managing all our resources so each will make its full contribution to a better United States—now and in the future.

United States Department of the Interior

NATIONAL PARK SERVICE
HISTORICAL HANDBOOK SERIES

Price lists of Park Service publications sold by the Government Printing Office may be obtained from the Superintendent of Documents, Washington, D.C. 20402.

☆ GPO:1978--266-764/10
For sale by the Superintendent of Documents,
U.S. Government Printing Office, Washington, DC 20402
Stock Number 024-005-00160-3
Catalog Number I 29.58:1/3